RALEIGH
RESTAURANT
GUIDE 2019

RESTAURANTS, BARS & CAFES

The Most Positively
Reviewed and Recommended
Restaurants in the City

EGP
Editorial

RALEIGH RESTAURANT GUIDE 2019
Best Rated Restaurants in Raleigh, North Carolina

© Jeanne A. Abrams, 2019
© E.G.P. Editorial, 2019

Printed in USA.

ISBN-13: 978-1720911869
ISBN-10: 172091186X

RALEIGH RESTAURANTS 2019

The Most Recommended Restaurants in Raleigh

This directory is dedicated to the Business Owners and Managers who provide the experience that the locals and tourists enjoy. Thanks you very much for all that you do and thank for being the "People Choice".

Thanks to everyone that posts their reviews online and the amazing reviews sites that make our life easier.

The places listed in this book are the most positively reviewed and recommended by locals and travelers from around the world.

Thank you for your time and enjoy the directory that is designed with locals and tourist in mind!

TOP 500
RESTAURANTS
Ranked from #1 to #500

#1
Guasaca
Cuisines: Venezuelan
Average price: Inexpensive
Address: 4025 Lake Boone Trl
Raleigh, NC 27607
Phone: (919) 322-4928

#2
Living Kitchen
Cuisines: Vegan, Vegetarian, Live/Raw Food
Average price: Modest
Address: 555 Fayetteville St
Raleigh, NC 27601
Phone: (919) 324-3515

#3
Bida Manda
Cuisines: Laotian, Asian Fusion, Thai
Average price: Modest
Address: 222 S Blount St
Raleigh, NC 27601
Phone: (919) 829-9999

#4
Stanbury
Cuisines: American
Average price: Expensive
Address: 938 N Blount St
Raleigh, NC 27604
Phone: (919) 977-4321

#5
Parkside
Cuisines: American
Average price: Modest
Address: 301 W Martin St
Raleigh, NC 27601
Phone: (984) 232-8969

#6
The Cowfish Sushi Burger Bar
Cuisines: Sushi Bar, Burgers
Average price: Modest
Address: 4208 Six Forks Rd
Raleigh, NC 27609
Phone: (919) 784-0400

#7
Mami Nora's
Cuisines: Peruvian
Average price: Inexpensive
Address: 2401 Wake Forest Rd
Raleigh, NC 27608
Phone: (919) 834-8572

#8
The Fiction Kitchen
Cuisines: Vegan, Vegetarian, Gluten-Free
Average price: Modest
Address: 428 S Dawson St
Raleigh, NC 27601
Phone: (919) 831-4177

#9
Glenwood Grill
Cuisines: American
Average price: Modest
Address: 2603-151 Glenwood Ave
Raleigh, NC 27608
Phone: (919) 782-3102

#10
Bad Daddy's Burger Bar
Cuisines: Burgers
Average price: Modest
Address: 111 Seaboard Ave
Raleigh, NC 27604
Phone: (919) 747-9163

#11
Tazza Kitchen Cameron Village
Cuisines: Pizza, American, Bar
Average price: Modest
Address: 432 Woodburn Rd
Raleigh, NC 27605
Phone: (919) 835-9463

#12
H Street Kitchen
Cuisines: Gastropub
Average price: Modest
Address: 2420 Hillsborough St
Raleigh, NC 27607
Phone: (919) 745-1983

#13
Monapita Mediterranean Grill
Cuisines: Mediterranean
Average price: Inexpensive
Address: 5260 Capital Blvd
Raleigh, NC 27616
Phone: (919) 431-6500

#14
Peri Brothers Pizza
Cuisines: Pizza, Italian, Pasta Shop
Average price: Inexpensive
Address: 7321 Six Forks Rd
Raleigh, NC 27615
Phone: (919) 844-6692

#15
Taste Small Plates | Wine Bar
Cuisines: American, Tapas/Small Plates
Average price: Modest
Address: 3048 Medlin Dr
Raleigh, NC 27607
Phone: (919) 322-0568

#16
Salt & Lime Cabo Grill
Cuisines: Seafood, Tex-Mex, Mexican
Average price: Modest
Address: 6006 Falls Of Neuse Rd
Raleigh, NC 27609
Phone: (919) 872-2230

#17
Mandolin
Cuisines: Southern, American
Average price: Expensive
Address: 2519 Fairview Rd
Raleigh, NC 27608
Phone: (919) 322-0365

#18
Soo Café
Cuisines: Korean, Chicken Wings
Average price: Modest
Address: 2815 Brentwood Rd
Raleigh, NC 27604
Phone: (919) 876-1969

#19
Trophy Brewing Company
Cuisines: Bar, Brewery, Pizza
Average price: Modest
Address: 827 W Morgan St
Raleigh, NC 27603
Phone: (919) 803-4849

#20
Second Empire Restaurant
Cuisines: American
Average price: Expensive
Address: 330 Hillsborough St
Raleigh, NC 27603
Phone: (919) 829-3663

#21
Oak & Dagger Public House
Cuisines: Brewery, Pub, American
Average price: Modest
Address: 18 Seaboard Ave
Raleigh, NC 27604
Phone: (919) 945-9382

#22
Neomonde Bakery & Deli
Cuisines: Bakery, Deli, Mediterranean
Average price: Inexpensive
Address: 3817 Beryl Rd
Raleigh, NC 27607
Phone: (919) 828-1628

#23
Devolve Moto
Cuisines: Outdoor Gear, Cafe, Fashion
Average price: Modest
Address: 304 Glenwood Ave
Raleigh, NC 27603
Phone: (919) 803-3257

#24
Bare Bones
Cuisines: Barbeque, Burgers, Sports Bar
Average price: Modest
Address: 301 Fayetteville St
Raleigh, NC 27601
Phone: (919) 825-0995

#25
Linus & Peppers
Cuisines: Salad, Sandwiches
Average price: Inexpensive
Address: 126 Salisbury St
Raleigh, NC 27601
Phone: (919) 833-3866

#26
J Betski's
Cuisines: German, Polish
Average price: Modest
Address: 10 W Franklin St
Raleigh, NC 27604
Phone: (919) 833-7999

#27
Night Kitchen Bakehouse & Cafe
Cuisines: Cafe, Bakery, Breakfast & Brunch
Average price: Inexpensive
Address: 10 W Franklin St
Raleigh, NC 27604
Phone: (984) 232-8907

#28
Gonza Tacos y Tequila
Cuisines: Mexican
Average price: Modest
Address: 7713-39 Lead Mine Rd
Raleigh, NC 27615
Phone: (919) 846-5478

#29
Ajisai Japanese Fusion
Cuisines: Japanese, Sushi Bar
Average price: Modest
Address: 427 Woodburn Rd
Raleigh, NC 27605
Phone: (919) 831-9907

#30
Beasley's Chicken & Honey
Cuisines: Southern, American
Average price: Modest
Address: 237 S Wilmington St
Raleigh, NC 27601
Phone: (919) 322-0127

#31
Plates Neighborhood Kitchen
Cuisines: American
Average price: Modest
Address: 301 Glenwood Ave
Raleigh, NC 27603
Phone: (919) 828-0018

#33
Taverna Agora
Cuisines: Greek, Bar
Average price: Modest
Address: 326 Hillsborough St
Raleigh, NC 27603
Phone: (919) 881-8333

#32
McAlister's Deli
Cuisines: Deli, Sandwiches, Salad
Average price: Inexpensive
Address: 5505 Capital Blvd
Raleigh, NC 27616
Phone: (919) 900-7846

#34
18 Seaboard
Cuisines: Southern, American
Average price: Modest
Address: 18 Seaboard Ave
Raleigh, NC 27604
Phone: (919) 861-4318

#35
Jose and Sons
Cuisines: American, Mexican
Average price: Modest
Address: 327 W Davie St
Raleigh, NC 27601
Phone: (919) 755-0556

#36
Standard Foods
Cuisines: American
Average price: Modest
Address: 205 E Franklin St
Raleigh, NC 27604
Phone: (919) 307-4652

#37
The Pit
Cuisines: Barbeque, American, Soul Food
Average price: Modest
Address: 328 W Davie St
Raleigh, NC 27601
Phone: (919) 890-4500

#38
Mitch's Tavern
Cuisines: Pub, American
Average price: Inexpensive
Address: 2426 Hillsborough St
Raleigh, NC 27607
Phone: (919) 821-7771

#39
Red Pepper Asian
Cuisines: Malaysian, Thai, Chinese
Average price: Modest
Address: 4121-109 New Bern Ave
Raleigh, NC 27610
Phone: (919) 594-1006

#40
Metro Diner
Cuisines: American, Diner
Average price: Modest
Address: 6325 Falls Of Neuse Rd
Raleigh, NC 27615
Phone: (919) 578-9053

#41
Manhattan Cafe
Cuisines: Cafe
Average price: Inexpensive
Address: 320 S Wilmington St
Raleigh, NC 27601
Phone: (919) 833-6105

#42
Hayes Barton Café & Dessertery
Cuisines: American, Desserts
Average price: Modest
Address: 2000 Fairview Rd
Raleigh, NC 27608
Phone: (919) 856-8551

#43
Wings Over Raleigh
Cuisines: Chicken Wings, Salad, Sandwiches
Average price: Inexpensive
Address: 2900 Hillsborough St
Raleigh, NC 27607
Phone: (919) 546-9111

#44
Bella Monica
Cuisines: Italian, Gluten-Free, Pizza
Average price: Modest
Address: 3121-103 Edwards Mill Rd
Raleigh, NC 27612
Phone: (919) 881-9778

#45
Chubby's Tacos
Cuisines: Mexican
Average price: Inexpensive
Address: 2444 Wycliff Rd
Raleigh, NC 27607
Phone: (919) 781-4480

#46
Garland
Cuisines: Asian Fusion, Cocktail Bar
Average price: Modest
Address: 14 W Martin St
Raleigh, NC 27601
Phone: (919) 833-6886

#47
David's Dumpling & Noodle Bar
Cuisines: Noodles
Average price: Modest
Address: 1900 Hillsborough St
Raleigh, NC 27607
Phone: (919) 239-4536

#48
Sassool
Cuisines: Mediterranean, Gluten-Free
Average price: Inexpensive
Address: 9650 Strickland Rd
Raleigh, NC 27615
Phone: (919) 847-2700

#49
Relish Café & Bar
Cuisines: Southern, Cafe, Burgers
Average price: Modest
Address: 5625 Creedmoor Rd
Raleigh, NC 27612
Phone: (919) 787-1855

#50
San Marcos Mexican Restaurant
Cuisines: Mexican, Seafood
Average price: Modest
Address: 5300 Homewood Banks Dr
Raleigh, NC 27612
Phone: (919) 803-4393

#51
Yard House
Cuisines: Bar, American, Vegetarian
Average price: Modest
Address: 4208 Six Forks Rd
Raleigh, NC 27609
Phone: (919) 881-2590

#52
Poole's
Cuisines: American
Average price: Modest
Address: 426 S McDowell St
Raleigh, NC 27601
Phone: (919) 832-4477

#53
Calavera Empanadas & Tequila
Cuisines: Latin American, Bar
Average price: Inexpensive
Address: 444 S Blount St
Raleigh, NC 27601
Phone: (919) 617-1661

#54
The Rockford
Cuisines: Sandwiches, American
Average price: Modest
Address: 320 1/2 Glenwood Ave
Raleigh, NC 27603
Phone: (919) 821-9020

#55
Pho Far East
Cuisines: Vietnamese
Average price: Modest
Address: 4011 Capital Blvd
Raleigh, NC 27604
Phone: (919) 876-8621

#56
Big Ed's City Market Restaurant
Cuisines: Breakfast & Brunch, Soul Food
Average price: Inexpensive
Address: 220 Wolfe St
Raleigh, NC 27601
Phone: (919) 836-9909

#57
Humble Pie
Cuisines: Breakfast & Brunch, American, Bar
Average price: Modest
Address: 317 S Harrington St
Raleigh, NC 27603
Phone: (919) 829-9222

#58
Kimbap
Cuisines: Korean, Gluten-Free, Salad
Average price: Modest
Address: 111 Seaboard Ave
Raleigh, NC 27604
Phone: (919) 900-8053

#59
Buku
Cuisines: Asian Fusion, Tapas, Thai
Average price: Modest
Address: 110 E Davie St
Raleigh, NC 27601
Phone: (919) 834-6963

#60
Taqueria El Toro
Cuisines: Mexican
Average price: Inexpensive
Address: 3601 Junction Blvd
Raleigh, NC 27603
Phone: (919) 661-5676

#61
Nashers Sandwich House
Cuisines: Sandwiches
Average price: Inexpensive
Address: 10630 Durant Rd
Raleigh, NC 27614
Phone: (984) 269-5099

#62
Irregardless Cafe & Catering
Cuisines: American, Vegetarian
Average price: Modest
Address: 901 W Morgan St
Raleigh, NC 27603
Phone: (919) 833-8898

#63
The Remedy Diner
Cuisines: Vegetarian, Sandwiches
Average price: Modest
Address: 137 E Hargett St
Raleigh, NC 27601
Phone: (919) 835-3553

#64
State of Beer
Cuisines: Bar, Sandwiches
Average price: Modest
Address: 401 Hillsborough St
Raleigh, NC 27603
Phone: (919) 546-9116

#65
Alpaca Peruvian Charcoal Chicken
Cuisines: Peruvian
Average price: Inexpensive
Address: 4614 Capital Blvd
Raleigh, NC 27604
Phone: (919) 713-0000

#66
More. Kitchen & Bar
Cuisines: Wine Bar, Tapas/Small Plates
Average price: Expensive
Address: 116 N West St
Raleigh, NC 27603
Phone: (919) 926-8415

#67
Fresh Levant Bistro
Cuisines: Mediterranean, Gluten-Free
Average price: Modest
Address: 8450 Honeycutt Rd
Raleigh, NC 27615
Phone: (984) 200-3999

#68
Firebirds Wood Fired Grill
Cuisines: Steakhouse, Seafood, Wine Bar
Average price: Modest
Address: 4350 Lassiter Rd
Raleigh, NC 27609
Phone: (919) 788-8778

#69
Tarbouch
Cuisines: Lebanese, Mediterranean
Average price: Inexpensive
Address: 5645 Creedmoor Rd
Raleigh, NC 27612
Phone: (919) 239-4408

#70
Chuck's
Cuisines: Burgers
Average price: Modest
Address: 237 S Wilmington St
Raleigh, NC 27601
Phone: (919) 322-0126

#71
Provenance
Cuisines: Southern, Bar, Breakfast & Brunch
Average price: Modest
Address: 120 E Martin St
Raleigh, NC 27601
Phone: (984) 269-5211

#72
Coquette Brasserie
Cuisines: French, Breakfast & Brunch
Average price: Modest
Address: 4351 The Circle at North HIlls
Raleigh, NC 27609
Phone: (919) 789-0606

#73
Bloomsbury Bistro
Cuisines: American
Average price: Expensive
Address: 509 W Whitaker Mill Rd
Raleigh, NC 27608
Phone: (919) 834-9011

#74
Kamado Grille
Cuisines: American, Seafood, Barbeque
Average price: Modest
Address: 832 Spring Forest Dr
Raleigh, NC 27609
Phone: (919) 803-3662

#75
Gravy
Cuisines: Italian, American
Average price: Modest
Address: 135 S Wilmington St
Raleigh, NC 27601
Phone: (919) 896-8513

#76
Gonza Tacos Y Tequila
Cuisines: Mexican
Average price: Modest
Address: 2100 Hillsborough St
Raleigh, NC 27607
Phone: (919) 268-8965

#77
The Oak
Cuisines: American
Average price: Modest
Address: 4035 Lake Boone Trail
Raleigh, NC 27607
Phone: (919) 787-9100

#78
NOFO @ The Pig
Cuisines: Specialty Food, American,
Breakfast & Brunch
Average price: Modest
Address: 2014 Fairview Rd
Raleigh, NC 27608
Phone: (919) 821-1240

#79
P.G. Werth's
Cuisines: American, Cafe, Specialty Food
Average price: Modest
Address: 927 W Morgan St
Raleigh, NC 27603
Phone: (984) 232-0415

#80
Rise Biscuits & Donuts
Cuisines: Donuts, Breakfast & Brunch
Average price: Inexpensive
Address: 6325 Falls of Neuse Rd
Raleigh, NC 27609
Phone: (984) 200-5751

#81
Clouds Brewing
Cuisines: Bar, Brewery, American
Average price: Modest
Address: 126 N West St
Raleigh, NC 27603
Phone: (919) 307-8335

#82
The Players Retreat
Cuisines: Sports Bar, American, Steakhouse
Average price: Modest
Address: 105 Oberlin Rd
Raleigh, NC 27605
Phone: (919) 755-9589

#83
Oak City Meatball Shoppe
Cuisines: Italian, Bar, American
Average price: Modest
Address: 180 E Davie St
Raleigh, NC 27601
Phone: (919) 714-9014

#84
MOD Pizza
Cuisines: Pizza, Fast Food
Average price: Inexpensive
Address: 2071 West Millbrook Rd
Raleigh, NC 27612
Phone: (919) 987-3668

#85
Vic's Italian Restaurant & Pizzeria
Cuisines: Pizza, Italian, Beer, Wine & Spirits
Average price: Modest
Address: 4035 Lake Boone Trail
Raleigh, NC 27607
Phone: (984) 200-9292

#86
The Daily Planet Cafe
Cuisines: Cafe, Sandwiches
Average price: Inexpensive
Address: 121 W Jones St
Raleigh, NC 27601
Phone: (919) 707-8060

#87
O'Malley's Pub & Restaurant
Cuisines: Pub, Irish
Average price: Inexpensive
Address: 5228 Hollyridge Dr
Raleigh, NC 27612
Phone: (919) 787-1234

#88
The Pharmacy Cafe
Cuisines: Cafe
Average price: Inexpensive
Address: 702 N Person St
Raleigh, NC 27604
Phone: (919) 977-3805

#89
Sitti
Cuisines: Middle Eastern
Average price: Modest
Address: 137 S Wilmington St
Raleigh, NC 27601
Phone: (919) 239-4070

#90
MoJoe's Burger Joint
Cuisines: Burgers
Average price: Inexpensive
Address: 620 Glenwood Ave
Raleigh, NC 27603
Phone: (919) 832-6799

#91
First Watch
Cuisines: American, Breakfast & Brunch
Average price: Modest
Address: 6109 Glenwood Ave
Raleigh, NC 27612
Phone: (919) 789-3347

#92
Oakwood Café
Cuisines: Cuban, Argentine
Average price: Modest
Address: 300 E Edenton St
Raleigh, NC 27601
Phone: (919) 828-5994

#93
ORO Restaurant & Lounge
Cuisines: Tapas, American, Lounge
Average price: Modest
Address: 18 E Martin St
Raleigh, NC 27601
Phone: (919) 239-4010

#94
The Mecca Restaurant
Cuisines: Diner
Average price: Inexpensive
Address: 13 E Martin St
Raleigh, NC 27601
Phone: (919) 832-5714

#95
Winston's Grille
Cuisines: American
Average price: Modest
Address: 6401 Falls of Neuse Rd
Raleigh, NC 27615
Phone: (919) 790-0700

#96
Raleigh Times Bar
Cuisines: Bar, American
Average price: Modest
Address: 14 E Hargett St
Raleigh, NC 27601
Phone: (919) 833-0999

#97
Despina's Cafe
Cuisines: Coffee & Tea, Sandwiches, Soup
Average price: Inexpensive
Address: 8369 Creedmoor Rd
Raleigh, NC 27613
Phone: (919) 848-5007

#98
Capital Club 16
Cuisines: American, Bar
Average price: Modest
Address: 16 W Martin St
Raleigh, NC 27601
Phone: (919) 747-9345

#99
The Station
Cuisines: Salad, Soup, American
Average price: Modest
Address: 701 N Person St
Raleigh, NC 27604
Phone: (919) 977-1567

#100
Busy Bee Cafe
Cuisines: American, Bar
Average price: Modest
Address: 225-100 S Wilmington St
Raleigh, NC 27601
Phone: (919) 424-7817

#101
My Way Tavern
Cuisines: American, Bar
Average price: Modest
Address: 522 Saint Marys St
Raleigh, NC 27605
Phone: (984) 444-2267

#102
Big Ed's North
Cuisines: Southern
Average price: Inexpensive
Address: 5009 Falls Of Neuse Rd
Raleigh, NC 27609
Phone: (919) 747-9533

#103
Vivace
Cuisines: Italian
Average price: Modest
Address: 4209 Lassiter Mill Rd
Raleigh, NC 27609
Phone: (919) 787-7747

#104
b.good
Cuisines: Fast Food
Average price: Modest
Address: 201 Park At N Hills St
Raleigh, NC 27609
Phone: (919) 916-5410

#105
Wade Park Cafe
Cuisines: Sandwiches, Breakfast & Brunch
Average price: Inexpensive
Address: 5430 Wade Park Blvd
Raleigh, NC 27607
Phone: (919) 859-5220

#106
Flying Saucer Draught Emporium
Cuisines: American, Pub
Average price: Modest
Address: 328 W Morgan St
Raleigh, NC 27601
Phone: (919) 821-7401

#107
Ole Time Barbecue
Cuisines: Barbeque
Average price: Inexpensive
Address: 6309 Hillsborough St
Raleigh, NC 27606
Phone: (919) 859-2544

#108
Death & Taxes
Cuisines: American, Soul Food
Average price: Exclusive
Address: 105 W Hargett St
Raleigh, NC 27601
Phone: (984) 242-0218

#109
Chuy's
Cuisines: Tex-Mex
Average price: Modest
Address: 4020 Market At North Hills St
Raleigh, NC 27609
Phone: (919) 571-2489

#110
Aggie's Grill Station
Cuisines: American
Average price: Inexpensive
Address: 3027-101 Capital Blvd
Raleigh, NC 27604
Phone: (919) 790-6688

#111
Driftwood Southern Kitchen
Cuisines: Southern
Average price: Modest
Address: 8460 Honeycutt Rd
Raleigh, NC 27615
Phone: (919) 977-8360

#112
Pam's Farm House
Cuisines: Southern, American
Average price: Inexpensive
Address: 5111 Western Blvd
Raleigh, NC 27606
Phone: (919) 859-9990

#113
Virgil's Original Taqueria
Cuisines: Mexican, Bar
Average price: Modest
Address: 126 S Salisbury St
Raleigh, NC 27601
Phone: (919) 833-3866

#114
Mi Cancun
Cuisines: Mexican
Average price: Modest
Address: 6675 Falls of Neuse Rd
Raleigh, NC 27615
Phone: (919) 977-3355

#115
Assaggio's
Cuisines: Italian, Pizza
Average price: Modest
Address: 3501 W Millbrook Rd
Raleigh, NC 27613
Phone: (919) 785-2088

#116
El Pollo Rico Restaurant
Cuisines: Mexican, Latin American, Spanish
Average price: Modest
Address: 3901 Capital Blvd
Raleigh, NC 27604
Phone: (919) 431-9985

#117
Margaux's Restaurant
Cuisines: American, French
Average price: Modest
Address: 8111 Creedmoor Rd
Raleigh, NC 27613
Phone: (919) 846-9846

#118
First Watch
Cuisines: Cafe, American
Average price: Modest
Address: 6320 Capital Blvd
Raleigh, NC 27616
Phone: (919) 900-8355

#119
Rye Bar & Southern Kitchen
Cuisines: Southern, American, Seafood
Average price: Modest
Address: 500 Fayetteville St
Raleigh, NC 27601
Phone: (919) 227-3370

#120
Lee's Kitchen
Cuisines: Caribbean, American
Average price: Modest
Address: 4638 Capital Blvd
Raleigh, NC 27604
Phone: (919) 872-7422

#121
Centro
Cuisines: Mexican, Gluten-Free
Average price: Modest
Address: 106 S Wilmington St
Raleigh, NC 27601
Phone: (919) 835-3593

#122
Kabab and Curry
Cuisines: Indian
Average price: Modest
Address: 2418 Hillsborough St
Raleigh, NC 27607
Phone: (919) 977-6974

#123
Clockwork
Cuisines: Bar, Pizza
Average price: Modest
Address: 519 W North St
Raleigh, NC 27603
Phone: (919) 307-3215

#124
Seaboard Cafe
Cuisines: American, Sandwiches, Caterer
Average price: Inexpensive
Address: 707 Semart Dr
Raleigh, NC 27604
Phone: (919) 821-7553

#125
Zoës Kitchen
Cuisines: Mediterranean, Greek
Average price: Inexpensive
Address: 141 - 112 Park At N Hills St
Raleigh, NC 27609
Phone: (919) 787-2820

#126
Jamaican Grille
Cuisines: Caribbean
Average price: Inexpensive
Address: 5500 Atlantic Springs Rd
Raleigh, NC 27616
Phone: (919) 873-0200

#127
Chopstix Gourmet and Sushi Bar
Cuisines: Chinese, Sushi Bar, Asian Fusion
Average price: Modest
Address: 5607 Creedmoor Rd
Raleigh, NC 27612
Phone: (919) 781-6268

#128
Got to Be NC Competition Dining
Cuisines: American, Festival
Average price: Expensive
Address: 1705 E Millbrook
Raleigh, NC 27609
Phone: (828) 265-9075

#129
Taza Grill
Cuisines: Greek, Mediterranean
Average price: Inexpensive
Address: 6325 Falls Of Neuse Rd
Raleigh, NC 27615
Phone: (919) 872-7161

#130
Indio
Cuisines: Indian, Seafood, Asian Fusion
Average price: Modest
Address: 222 Glenwood Ave
Raleigh, NC 27603
Phone: (919) 322-2760

#131
North Ridge Pub
Cuisines: Pub, American
Average price: Modest
Address: 6010 Falls Of Neuse Rd
Raleigh, NC 27609
Phone: (919) 790-9125

#132
Saltwater Seafood & Fry Shack
Cuisines: Seafood, Seafood Market
Average price: Inexpensive
Address: 4 Fenton St
Raleigh, NC 27604
Phone: (919) 834-1813

#133
Tasty 8's
Cuisines: Hot Dogs, American
Average price: Inexpensive
Address: 121 Fayetteville St
Raleigh, NC 27601
Phone: (919) 307-8558

#134
Brookside Market & Pizza
Cuisines: Italian, Pizza, Deli
Average price: Inexpensive
Address: 1000 Brookside Dr
Raleigh, NC 27604
Phone: (919) 828-3404

#135
State Farmers Market Restaurant
Cuisines: Southern, Sandwiches
Average price: Inexpensive
Address: 1240 Farmers Market Dr
Raleigh, NC 27603
Phone: (919) 755-1550

#136
Gringo A Go-Go
Cuisines: Mexican
Average price: Modest
Address: 100 N Person St
Raleigh, NC 27601
Phone: (919) 977-1438

#137
Bahama Breeze
Cuisines: Seafood, Caribbean, Bar
Average price: Modest
Address: 3309 Wake Forest Dr
Raleigh, NC 27609
Phone: (919) 872-6330

#138
BURGERFI
Cuisines: Burgers, Hot Dogs, American
Average price: Modest
Address: 3004 Wake Forest Rd
Raleigh, NC 27609
Phone: (919) 999-3700

#139
Ni Asian Kitchen
Cuisines: Chinese, Thai, Malaysian
Average price: Modest
Address: 8817 Six Forks Rd
Raleigh, NC 27615
Phone: (919) 916-5106

#140
Latin Quarters
Cuisines: Bar, Latin American
Average price: Modest
Address: 7335 Six Forks Rd
Raleigh, NC 27615
Phone: (919) 900-8333

#141
Sosta Café
Cuisines: Coffee & Tea, Sandwiches
Average price: Inexpensive
Address: 130 E Davie St
Raleigh, NC 27601
Phone: (919) 833-1006

#142
Lynnwood Grill & Brewing Concern
Cuisines: Pizza, Bar, American
Average price: Modest
Address: 4821 Grove Barton Rd
Raleigh, NC 27613
Phone: (919) 785-0043

#143
Another Broken Egg Cafe
Cuisines: American,
Breakfast & Brunch, Cafe
Average price: Modest
Address: 160 Park at N Hills
Raleigh, NC 27609
Phone: (919) 307-8195

#144
Al Baraka Market and Grill
Cuisines: Mediterranean, Bakery
Average price: Inexpensive
Address: 3815 Hillsborough St
Raleigh, NC 27607
Phone: (919) 838-5155

#145
Pho Pho Pho
Cuisines: Vietnamese, Soup
Average price: Modest
Address: 510 Glenwood Ave
Raleigh, NC 27603
Phone: (919) 322-1433

#146
Watkins Grill
Cuisines: Breakfast & Brunch, American
Average price: Inexpensive
Address: 1625 Wake Forest Rd
Raleigh, NC 27604
Phone: (919) 834-0467

#147
**42nd Street Oyster Bar
& Seafood Grill**
Cuisines: Seafood, Lounge
Average price: Modest
Address: 508 W Jones St
Raleigh, NC 27603
Phone: (919) 831-2811

#148
Brio Tuscan Grille
Cuisines: Italian, Pizza, Cocktail Bar
Average price: Modest
Address: 4325 Glenwood Ave
Raleigh, NC 27612
Phone: (919) 881-2048

#149
Angus Barn
Cuisines: Steakhouse, Lounge, American
Average price: Expensive
Address: 9401 Glenwood Ave
Raleigh, NC 27617
Phone: (919) 781-2444

#150
Tupelo Honey Cafe
Cuisines: Southern, American
Average price: Modest
Address: 425 Oberlin Rd
Raleigh, NC 27605
Phone: (919) 723-9353

#151
Lilly's Pizza
Cuisines: Pizza
Average price: Modest
Address: 1813 Glenwood Ave
Raleigh, NC 27608
Phone: (919) 833-0226

#152
Vivo Ristorante Pizzeria
Cuisines: Italian, Pizza
Average price: Modest
Address: 7400 Six Forks Rd
Raleigh, NC 27615
Phone: (919) 845-6700

#153
Kai Sushi and Sake Bar
Cuisines: Japanese, Sushi Bar
Average price: Modest
Address: 7713 Lead Mine Rd
Raleigh, NC 27615
Phone: (919) 870-4923

#154
Rise Biscuits Donuts
Cuisines: Donuts, Bakery
Average price: Inexpensive
Address: 530 Daniels St
Raleigh, NC 27605
Phone: (984) 200-6966

#155
Godavari Indian Restaurant
Cuisines: Indian, Buffet
Average price: Modest
Address: 9650 Strickland Rd
Raleigh, NC 27615
Phone: (919) 847-1984

#156
Poppyseed Market
Cuisines: Deli, Wine Bar, Pizza
Average price: Modest
Address: 8801 Leadmine Rd
Raleigh, NC 27615
Phone: (919) 870-4997

#157
Sopranos Grill
Cuisines: Italian, American
Average price: Modest
Address: 1030 N Rogers Ln
Raleigh, NC 27610
Phone: (919) 827-8848

#158
Vinos Finos Tapas and Wine Bar
Cuisines: Wine Bar, Tapas Bar
Average price: Modest
Address: 8450 Honeycutt Rd
Raleigh, NC 27615
Phone: (919) 747-9233

#159
The Morning Times
Cuisines: Coffee & Tea, Bakery
Average price: Inexpensive
Address: 10 E Hargett St
Raleigh, NC 27601
Phone: (919) 836-1204

#160
Flying Burrito
Cuisines: Tex-Mex, Bar, Mexican
Average price: Modest
Address: 4800 Grove Barton Rd
Raleigh, NC 27613
Phone: (919) 785-2734

#161
Joule Coffee & Table
Cuisines: Coffee & Tea, American
Average price: Modest
Address: 223 S Wilmington St
Raleigh, NC 27601
Phone: (919) 424-7422

#162
DeMo's Pizzeria & Deli
Cuisines: Pizza, Deli
Average price: Inexpensive
Address: 222 Glenwood Ave
Raleigh, NC 27603
Phone: (919) 754-1050

#163
Duck Donuts
Cuisines: Donuts, Breakfast & Brunch
Average price: Inexpensive
Address: 8323 Creedmoor Road
Raleigh, NC 27613
Phone: (919) 847-3800

#164
Cristo's NY Style Pizza
Cuisines: Pizza
Average price: Modest
Address: 1302 E Millbrook Rd
Raleigh, NC 27609
Phone: (919) 872-6797

#165
Saint Jacques
Cuisines: French, Wine Bar
Average price: Expensive
Address: 6112 Falls Of Neuse Rd
Raleigh, NC 27609
Phone: (919) 862-2770

#166
Side Street Restaurant
Cuisines: Sandwiches, American
Average price: Inexpensive
Address: 225 N Bloodworth St
Raleigh, NC 27601
Phone: (919) 828-4927

#167
Hero's Pub & Sandwich Shop
Cuisines: Arcades, Pub, Sandwiches
Average price: Modest
Address: 7440 Six Forks Rd
Raleigh, NC 27615
Phone: (919) 706-5150

#168
Sono
Cuisines: Japanese, Sushi Bar
Average price: Modest
Address: 319 Fayetteville St
Raleigh, NC 27601
Phone: (919) 521-5328

#169
Shaba Shabu
Cuisines: Japanese, Thai, Sushi Bar
Average price: Modest
Address: 3080 Wake Forest Rd
Raleigh, NC 27609
Phone: (919) 501-7755

#170
Tenko Japan
Cuisines: Japanese
Average price: Inexpensive
Address: 4040 Ed Dr
Raleigh, NC 27612
Phone: (919) 781-5181

#171
Pieology Pizzeria
Cuisines: Pizza
Average price: Inexpensive
Address: 4158 Main At North Hills
Raleigh, NC 27609
Phone: (919) 803-5860

#172
Aladdin's Eatery
Cuisines: Mediterranean, Vegan, Gluten-Free
Average price: Modest
Address: 8201 Brier Creek Pkwy
Raleigh, NC 27617
Phone: (919) 806-5700

#173
Cariokos Rotisserie Chicken
Cuisines: Peruvian, Latin American
Average price: Inexpensive
Address: 1601-43 Cross Link Rd
Raleigh, NC 27610
Phone: (919) 755-5727

#174
Waraji Japanese Restaurant
Cuisines: Japanese, Sushi Bar
Average price: Modest
Address: 5910 Duraleigh Rd
Raleigh, NC 27612
Phone: (919) 783-1883

#175
Frank's Pizza & Italian Restaurant
Cuisines: Pizza, Italian
Average price: Modest
Address: 2030 New Bern Ave
Raleigh, NC 27610
Phone: (984) 221-1398

#176
Barry's Cafe
Cuisines: Burgers, American
Average price: Inexpensive
Address: 2851 Jones Franklin Rd
Raleigh, NC 27606
Phone: (919) 859-3555

#177
Fu Kee Express
Cuisines: Chinese
Average price: Inexpensive
Address: 6320 Capital Blvd
Raleigh, NC 27616
Phone: (919) 872-2661

#178
Groucho's Deli of Raleigh
Cuisines: Sandwiches, Deli
Average price: Inexpensive
Address: 10 Horne St
Raleigh, NC 27607
Phone: (919) 977-7747

#179
Taza Grill
Cuisines: Mediterranean, Greek
Average price: Inexpensive
Address: 10940 Raven Ridge Rd
Raleigh, NC 27614
Phone: (919) 845-7772

#180
Backyard Bistro
Cuisines: American, Sports Bar
Average price: Modest
Address: 1235 Hurricane Alley Way
Raleigh, NC 27607
Phone: (919) 851-6203

#181
Chow Pizza Bar
Cuisines: Pizza, Sports Bar, Burgers
Average price: Inexpensive
Address: 8311 Creedmoor Rd
Raleigh, NC 27613
Phone: (919) 841-4995

#182
Pearl Chinese Restaurant
Cuisines: Chinese, Seafood, Soup
Average price: Inexpensive
Address: 3215 Avent Ferry Rd
Raleigh, NC 27606
Phone: (919) 233-8776

#183
Los Cuates
Cuisines: Mexican
Average price: Inexpensive
Address: 4524 Old Wake Forest Rd
Raleigh, NC 27609
Phone: (919) 872-6012

#184
Don Beto's Tacos
Cuisines: Mexican
Average price: Inexpensive
Address: 421 Chapanoke Rd
Raleigh, NC 27603
Phone: (919) 977-1071

#185
Seoul Garden Restaurant
Cuisines: Korean
Average price: Modest
Address: 4701 Atlantic Ave
Raleigh, NC 27604
Phone: (919) 850-9984

#186
Lunch Box Deli
Cuisines: Deli
Average price: Inexpensive
Address: 2816 Trawick Rd Ste 105
Raleigh, NC 27604
Phone: (919) 872-7882

#187
Thai House
Cuisines: Thai
Average price: Modest
Address: 1408 Hardimont Rd
Raleigh, NC 27609
Phone: (919) 878-3379

#188
Pho Super 9
Cuisines: Vietnamese
Average price: Modest
Address: 6401 Triangle Plantation Dr
Raleigh, NC 27616
Phone: (919) 878-1599

#189
Big Al's BBQ
Cuisines: Barbeque
Average price: Modest
Address: 2920 Forestville Rd
Raleigh, NC 27616
Phone: (919) 217-0653

#190
Burger 21
Cuisines: Burgers, Salad, Hot Dogs
Average price: Modest
Address: 6196 Falls Of Neuse Rd
Raleigh, NC 27609
Phone: (919) 900-8807

#191
Tenko Japan
Cuisines: Japanese
Average price: Inexpensive
Address: 6325-67 Falls of Neuse Rd
Raleigh, NC 27609
Phone: (919) 876-4545

#192
Mum's Jamaican Restaurant
Cuisines: Caribbean
Average price: Modest
Address: 3901 Capital Blvd
Raleigh, NC 27604
Phone: (919) 615-2332

#193
TLC Wings & Grill
Cuisines: Chicken Wings, Pizza, Sandwiches
Average price: Modest
Address: 805 W Peace St
Raleigh, NC 27605
Phone: (919) 834-8292

#194
The Pickled Onion
Cuisines: Sports Bar, American, Karaoke
Average price: Modest
Address: 7901 Falls of Neuse Rd
Raleigh, NC 27615
Phone: (919) 848-4161

#195
Smashburger
Cuisines: Burgers
Average price: Inexpensive
Address: 6679 Falls of Neuse Rd
Raleigh, NC 27615
Phone: (919) 870-9230

#196
Serena Sicilian Influenced Cucina
Cuisines: Italian, Wine Bar, Mediterranean
Average price: Modest
Address: 7456 Creedmoor Rd
Raleigh, NC 27613
Phone: (919) 900-7685

#197
Manchester's Grill
Cuisines: Pizza
Average price: Modest
Address: 9101 Leesville Rd
Raleigh, NC 27613
Phone: (919) 676-3310

#198
Spring Rolls
Cuisines: Asian Fusion, Chinese, Sushi Bar
Average price: Modest
Address: 5433 Wade Park Boulevard
Raleigh, NC 27607
Phone: (919) 803-1118

#199
Cafe Tiramisu
Cuisines: Italian
Average price: Modest
Address: 6008 Falls Of Neuse Rd
Raleigh, NC 27609
Phone: (919) 790-1006

#200
Tijuana Flats
Cuisines: Mexican, Tex-Mex
Average price: Inexpensive
Address: 1310 E. Millbrook Rd.
Raleigh, NC 27609
Phone: (919) 790-6409

#201
The Knight Kaffee
Cuisines: Mediterranean, Lebanese
Average price: Inexpensive
Address: 1803 Glenwood Ave
Raleigh, NC 27608
Phone: (919) 834-8337

#202
The Big Easy
Cuisines: Cajun/Creole
Average price: Modest
Address: 222 Fayetteville St
Raleigh, NC 27601
Phone: (919) 832-6082

#203
Mura
Cuisines: Sushi Bar, Japanese
Average price: Modest
Address: 4121 Main at N Hill,Ste 110
Raleigh, NC 27609
Phone: (919) 781-7887

#204
Tacos Y Mariscos Vallarta
Cuisines: Mexican
Average price: Modest
Address: 3177 Capital Blvd
Raleigh, NC 27604
Phone: (919) 790-2696

#205
Tribeca Tavern
Cuisines: American, Burgers, Sandwiches
Average price: Modest
Address: 6004 Falls Of Neuse Rd
Raleigh, NC 27609
Phone: (919) 790-9992

#206
Justin's Grill
Cuisines: Mediterranean, Sandwiches
Average price: Inexpensive
Address: 1322 E Millbrook Rd
Raleigh, NC 27609
Phone: (919) 876-2007

#207
Mr. Wonderfuls Chicken & Waffles
Cuisines: Chicken Wings, Southern
Average price: Modest
Address: 3587 Maitland Dr
Raleigh, NC 27610
Phone: (919) 896-6063

#208
Clyde Cooper's Barbecue
Cuisines: Barbeque
Average price: Inexpensive
Address: 327 S Wilmington St
Raleigh, NC 27601
Phone: (919) 832-7614

#209
The Point at Glenwood
Cuisines: Bar, American, Breakfast & Brunch
Average price: Modest
Address: 1626 Glenwood Ave
Raleigh, NC 27608
Phone: (919) 755-1007

#210
Moonlight Pizza Company
Cuisines: Pizza
Average price: Modest
Address: 615 W Morgan St
Raleigh, NC 27603
Phone: (919) 755-9133

#211
Jack's Seafood & Soul Food
Cuisines: Seafood, Southern, Soul Food
Average price: Inexpensive
Address: 1516 New Bern Ave
Raleigh, NC 27610
Phone: (919) 755-1551

#212
Tropical Picken Chicken Raleigh
Cuisines: Dominican, Puerto Rican, Cuban
Average price: Modest
Address: 404 E Six Forks Rd
Raleigh, NC 27609
Phone: (919) 703-0661

#213
Twisted Fork
Cuisines: American
Average price: Modest
Address: 3571 Sumner Blvd
Raleigh, NC 27616
Phone: (919) 792-2535

#214
Whiskey Kitchen
Cuisines: Southern, Cocktail Bar
Average price: Modest
Address: 201 W Martin St
Raleigh, NC 27601
Phone: (919) 803-3181

#215
Carolina Sushi & Roll
Cuisines: Sushi Bar, Japanese
Average price: Modest
Address: 5951 Poyner Village Pkwy
Raleigh, NC 27616
Phone: (919) 981-5835

#216
Berkeley Cafe
Cuisines: Bar, Burgers, Sandwiches
Average price: Inexpensive
Address: 217 W Martin St
Raleigh, NC 27601
Phone: (919) 828-9190

#217
Spring Cafe
Cuisines: Sandwiches, American
Average price: Inexpensive
Address: 2900 Spring Forest Rd
Raleigh, NC 27616
Phone: (919) 977-3679

#218
Babylon Restaurant
Cuisines: Moroccan, Venue & Event Space
Average price: Modest
Address: 309 N Dawson St
Raleigh, NC 27603
Phone: (919) 838-8595

#219
Mia Francesca
Cuisines: Italian, Breakfast & Brunch
Average price: Modest
Address: 4100 Main at North Hills St
Raleigh, NC 27609
Phone: (919) 278-1525

#220
The Roast Grill
Cuisines: Hot Dogs
Average price: Inexpensive
Address: 7 S West St
Raleigh, NC 27603
Phone: (919) 832-8292

#221
Casa Carbone Ristorante Italiano
Cuisines: Italian
Average price: Modest
Address: 6019 Glenwood Ave
Raleigh, NC 27612
Phone: (919) 781-8750

#222
Hibernian Restaurant & Pub
Cuisines: Irish, Pub
Average price: Modest
Address: 311 Glenwood Ave
Raleigh, NC 27603
Phone: (919) 833-2258

#223
Piola
Cuisines: Pizza, Italian
Average price: Modest
Address: 141 Park at North Hills St
Raleigh, NC 27609
Phone: (919) 758-8059

#224
Sullivan's Steakhouse
Cuisines: Bar, Steakhouse
Average price: Expensive
Address: 414 Glenwood Ave
Raleigh, NC 27603
Phone: (919) 833-2888

#225
Wakefield Tavern
Cuisines: American, Pizza, Sandwiches
Average price: Modest
Address: 13200 Falls of Neuse Rd
Raleigh, NC 27614
Phone: (919) 554-0673

#226
Boondini's Sandwich Superstore
Cuisines: Sandwiches
Average price: Inexpensive
Address: 7403 Six Forks Rd
Raleigh, NC 27615
Phone: (919) 848-2487

#227
The Piper's Tavern
Cuisines: American
Average price: Modest
Address: 8304 Falls of Neuse Rd
Raleigh, NC 27615
Phone: (919) 676-7413

#228
Casa San Carlo
Cuisines: Italian, Seafood, Buffet
Average price: Modest
Address: 9660 Falls Of Neuse Rd
Raleigh, NC 27615
Phone: (919) 676-3262

#229
Red Dragon Chinese Restaurant
Cuisines: Chinese
Average price: Modest
Address: 2513 Fairview Rd
Raleigh, NC 27608
Phone: (919) 782-1102

#230
Village Draft House
Cuisines: Bar, Burgers, American
Average price: Modest
Address: 428 Daniels St
Raleigh, NC 27605
Phone: (919) 833-1373

#231
Cameron Bar and Grill
Cuisines: Bar, American
Average price: Modest
Address: 2019 Clark Ave
Raleigh, NC 27605
Phone: (919) 755-2231

#232
El Tapatio Mexican Restaurant
Cuisines: Mexican
Average price: Inexpensive
Address: 4511 New Bern Ave
Raleigh, NC 27610
Phone: (919) 255-9161

#233
Sawasdee Thai Restaurant
Cuisines: Thai
Average price: Modest
Address: 3601 Capital Blvd
Raleigh, NC 27604
Phone: (919) 878-0049

#234
PDQ
Cuisines: Sandwiches, Salad
Average price: Inexpensive
Address: 6305 Falls of Neuse Rd
Raleigh, NC 27615
Phone: (919) 803-1171

#235
Wicked Taco Raleigh
Cuisines: Mexican
Average price: Inexpensive
Address: 3928 Western Blvd
Raleigh, NC 27606
Phone: (919) 322-0446

#236
Nur Mediterranean Deli & Market
Cuisines: Grocery, Mediterranean
Average price: Inexpensive
Address: 2233 Avent Ferry Rd
Raleigh, NC 27606
Phone: (919) 828-1523

#237
The Wild Cook's Indian Grill
Cuisines: Indian
Average price: Modest
Address: 3212 Hillsborough St
Raleigh, NC 27607
Phone: (984) 232-8530

#238
Benelux Coffee
Cuisines: Coffee & Tea, Bakery
Average price: Inexpensive
Address: 402 Oberlin Rd
Raleigh, NC 27605
Phone: (919) 900-8294

#239
Sushi-Thai Restaurant
Cuisines: Sushi Bar, Thai, Japanese
Average price: Modest
Address: 2434 Wycliff Rd
Raleigh, NC 27613
Phone: (919) 789-8180

#240
Mo-Te Vietnamese Restaurant
Cuisines: Vietnamese
Average price: Inexpensive
Address: 3901-163 Capital Blvd
Raleigh, NC 27604
Phone: (919) 872-3561

#241
Freshii
Cuisines: Vegetarian, Salad, Juice Bar
Average price: Inexpensive
Address: 2316 Hillsborough St
Raleigh, NC 27607
Phone: (919) 424-7900

#242
Mellow Mushroom
Cuisines: Pizza, Bar, Sandwiches
Average price: Modest
Address: 601 W Peace St
Raleigh, NC 27605
Phone: (919) 832-3499

#243
Village Deli & Grill - Lake Boone Trail
Cuisines: Deli, American, Sandwiches
Average price: Modest
Address: 2500 Wycliff Rd
Raleigh, NC 27607
Phone: (919) 803-1245

#244
Taj Mahal
Cuisines: Indian
Average price: Modest
Address: 6611 Falls of Neuse Rd
Raleigh, NC 27615
Phone: (919) 848-2262

#245
Gino's Pizza
Cuisines: Pizza
Average price: Inexpensive
Address: 6260 Glenwood Ave
Raleigh, NC 27612
Phone: (919) 783-7555

#246
Imperial Garden Chinese Restaurant
Cuisines: Chinese
Average price: Modest
Address: 7713 Lead Mine Rd
Raleigh, NC 27615
Phone: (919) 846-1988

#247
The Capital Grille
Cuisines: Steakhouse, Wine Bar, Seafood
Average price: Expensive
Address: 4242 Six Forks Rd
Raleigh, NC 27609
Phone: (919) 787-3901

#248
Jubala Village Coffee
Cuisines: Cafe, Sandwiches
Average price: Inexpensive
Address: 2100 Hillsborough Street
Raleigh, NC 27607
Phone: (919) 758-8330

#249
Community Deli
Cuisines: Deli, Burgers, Hot Dogs
Average price: Inexpensive
Address: 901 Oberlin Rd
Raleigh, NC 27605
Phone: (919) 896-6810

#250
Anvil's Cheesesteaks
Cuisines: Cheesesteaks
Average price: Inexpensive
Address: 2893 Jones Franklin Rd
Raleigh, NC 27606
Phone: (919) 854-0558

#251
The Flying Biscuit
Cuisines: American, Breakfast & Brunch
Average price: Modest
Address: 2016 Clark Ave
Raleigh, NC 27605
Phone: (919) 833-6924

#252
Village Deli and Grill
Cuisines: Deli, American
Average price: Modest
Address: 500 Daniels St
Raleigh, NC 27605
Phone: (919) 828-1428

#253
Sunflowers Cafe
Cuisines: Sandwiches, American, Vegetarian
Average price: Inexpensive
Address: 8 W Peace St
Raleigh, NC 27603
Phone: (919) 833-4676

#254
Hangover Grill
Cuisines: Burgers, Sandwiches, American
Average price: Inexpensive
Address: 2908 Hillsborough St
Raleigh, NC 27607
Phone: (984) 200-1202

#255
Max's Pizza & Grill
Cuisines: Pizza
Average price: Inexpensive
Address: 5609 Creedmoor Rd
Raleigh, NC 27612
Phone: (919) 783-6565

#256
Hako Japanese Restaurant
Cuisines: Sushi Bar, Japanese
Average price: Modest
Address: 2603-155 Glenwood Ave
Raleigh, NC 27608
Phone: (919) 235-0589

#257
Jimmy V's Osteria & Bar
Cuisines: Bar, American, Italian
Average price: Modest
Address: 420 Fayetteville St
Raleigh, NC 27601
Phone: (919) 256-1451

#258
Brixx Wood Fired Pizza
Cuisines: Pizza
Average price: Modest
Address: 402 Oberlin Rd
Raleigh, NC 27605
Phone: (919) 723-9370

#259
The Alley
Cuisines: Bowling, American
Average price: Inexpensive
Address: 2512 Hillsborough St
Raleigh, NC 27607
Phone: (919) 832-3533

#260
Cantina 18
Cuisines: Tex-Mex
Average price: Modest
Address: 433 Daniels St
Raleigh, NC 27605
Phone: (919) 835-9911

#261
Spring Rolls
Cuisines: Asian Fusion
Average price: Modest
Address: 4361 Lassiter At N Hills Ave
Raleigh, NC 27609
Phone: (919) 783-8180

#262
Dos Taquitos Xoco
Cuisines: Mexican
Average price: Modest
Address: 410 Glenwood Ave
Raleigh, NC 27603
Phone: (919) 835-9010

#263
Armadillo Grill
Cuisines: Mexican, Tex-Mex
Average price: Inexpensive
Address: 439 Glenwood Ave
Raleigh, NC 27603
Phone: (919) 546-0555

#264
River Pub
Cuisines: American, Pub
Average price: Modest
Address: 10940 Raven Ridge Rd
Raleigh, NC 27614
Phone: (919) 900-8302

#265
Shish Kabob
Cuisines: Mediterranean, Greek
Average price: Inexpensive
Address: 438 Fayetteville St
Raleigh, NC 27601
Phone: (919) 833-4005

#266
Hibachi 88
Cuisines: Japanese, Asian Fusion
Average price: Modest
Address: 3416-100 Poole Rd
Raleigh, NC 27610
Phone: (919) 231-1688

#267
PhoXpress
Cuisines: Vietnamese, Asian Fusion
Average price: Inexpensive
Address: 7841 Alexander Pl
Raleigh, NC 27617
Phone: (919) 400-4100

#268
The Village Grill
Cuisines: American, Burgers, Sandwiches
Average price: Modest
Address: 8470 Honeycutt Rd
Raleigh, NC 27615
Phone: (919) 890-5340

#269
Papa's Pizza & Wings
Cuisines: Pizza, Italian, American
Average price: Modest
Address: 5800-111 Duraleigh Rd
Raleigh, NC 27612
Phone: (919) 783-7373

#270
Hibachi 101
Cuisines: Japanese
Average price: Inexpensive
Address: 7870 Alexander Promenade Pl
Raleigh, NC 27617
Phone: (919) 596-2888

#271
Sawasdee Thai Restaurant & Bar
Cuisines: Thai, Ramen, Sushi Bar
Average price: Modest
Address: 6204 Glenwood Ave
Raleigh, NC 27612
Phone: (919) 781-7599

#272
Bonefish Grill
Cuisines: Seafood
Average price: Modest
Address: 4421 6 Forks Rd
Raleigh, NC 27609
Phone: (919) 782-5127

#273
Flame Kabob
Cuisines: Persian/Iranian
Average price: Modest
Address: 7961 Skyland Ridge Pkwy
Raleigh, NC 27617
Phone: (919) 596-2525

#274
Flights Restaurant & Lounge
Cuisines: American, Lounge
Average price: Expensive
Address: 4100 Main At North Hills St
Raleigh, NC 27609
Phone: (919) 278-1478

#275
Fox and Hound Pub & Grille
Cuisines: Sports Bar, American
Average price: Modest
Address: 4158 Main N Hills St
Raleigh, NC 27609
Phone: (919) 781-4495

#276
Saints & Scholars
Cuisines: Irish, Pub
Average price: Modest
Address: 909 Spring Forest Rd
Raleigh, NC 27609
Phone: (919) 878-8828

#277
Zoes Kitchen
Cuisines: Mediterranean, Sandwiches, Salad
Average price: Inexpensive
Address: 1028 Oberlin Rd
Raleigh, NC 27605
Phone: (919) 838-0909

#278
Polish Market Polonez
Cuisines: Grocery, Hungarian, Ukrainian
Average price: Modest
Address: 5440 Atlantic Springs Rd
Raleigh, NC 27616
Phone: (919) 790-1466

#279
Cafe Carolina and Bakery
Cuisines: Bakery, Sandwiches, Cafe
Average price: Inexpensive
Address: 401 Daniels St
Raleigh, NC 27605
Phone: (919) 457-1633

#280
Five Star Restaurant
Cuisines: Chinese, Bar, Diner
Average price: Modest
Address: 511 W Hargett St
Raleigh, NC 27603
Phone: (919) 833-3311

#281
Buffalo Brothers
Cuisines: Sports Bar, American
Average price: Modest
Address: 4025 Lake Boone Trl
Raleigh, NC 27607
Phone: (919) 782-4949

#282
Sushi Tsune
Cuisines: Sushi Bar
Average price: Modest
Address: 3417 Hillsborough St
Raleigh, NC 27607
Phone: (919) 833-7768

#283
Dos Taquitos
Cuisines: Mexican
Average price: Modest
Address: 6101 Glenwood Ave
Raleigh, NC 27612
Phone: (919) 787-3373

#284
Papa's Pizza & Subs
Cuisines: Pizza, Salad, Sandwiches
Average price: Inexpensive
Address: 7713 Lead Mine Rd
Raleigh, NC 27615
Phone: (919) 847-8777

#285
Earp's Seafood
Cuisines: Seafood Market, Seafood
Average price: Modest
Address: 1414 S Saunders St
Raleigh, NC 27603
Phone: (919) 833-3158

#286
Donatos Seaboard
Cuisines: Pizza, Salad, Sandwiches
Average price: Modest
Address: 111 Seaboard Ave
Raleigh, NC 27604
Phone: (919) 828-5111

#287
La Rancherita
Cuisines: Mexican
Average price: Modest
Address: 4325 Glenwood Ave
Raleigh, NC 27612
Phone: (919) 785-1951

#288
Hibernian Restaurant & Pub
Cuisines: Irish, Pub
Average price: Modest
Address: 8021 Falls of Neuse Rd
Raleigh, NC 27615
Phone: (919) 803-0290

#289
510 Tavern
Cuisines: Sports Bar, Gastropub
Average price: Modest
Address: 510 Glenwood Ave
Raleigh, NC 27603
Phone: (919) 307-4778

#290
Cafe Buongiorno's
Cuisines: Italian, Sandwiches, Bakery
Average price: Inexpensive
Address: 3607 Falls River Ave
Raleigh, NC 27614
Phone: (919) 896-7459

#291
Jasmin Mediterranean
Cuisines: Mediterranean, Greek, Lebanese
Average price: Inexpensive
Address: 3801 Hillsborough St
Raleigh, NC 27607
Phone: (919) 835-1626

#292
Red Monkey Tavern
Cuisines: American, Gastropub
Average price: Modest
Address: 4325 Glenwood Ave
Raleigh, NC 27612
Phone: (919) 896-7412

#293
Third Place Coffee House
Cuisines: Coffee & Tea, Sandwiches, Bagels
Average price: Inexpensive
Address: 1811 Glenwood Ave
Raleigh, NC 27608
Phone: (919) 834-6566

#294
Hibachi Asian Diner
Cuisines: Chinese
Average price: Inexpensive
Address: 2004 New Bern Ave
Raleigh, NC 27610
Phone: (919) 594-1772

#295
Randy's Pizza
Cuisines: Pizza
Average price: Inexpensive
Address: 2458 Wycliff Rd
Raleigh, NC 27607
Phone: (919) 322-5990

#296
Golden Palace
Cuisines: Dim Sum, Cantonese
Average price: Modest
Address: 4420 Capital Blvd
Raleigh, NC 27604
Phone: (919) 900-7665

#297
Rey's Restaurant
Cuisines: Seafood, Steakhouse, American
Average price: Expensive
Address: 1130 Buck Jones Rd
Raleigh, NC 27606
Phone: (919) 380-0122

#298
Jamaican Jerk Masters
Cuisines: Caribbean
Average price: Inexpensive
Address: 3110 New Bern Ave
Raleigh, NC 27610
Phone: (919) 803-7407

#299
The Luxury Box
Cuisines: American, Sports Bar
Average price: Modest
Address: 8511 Cantilever Way
Raleigh, NC 27613
Phone: (919) 900-7955

#300
Abyssinia Ethiopian Restaurant
Cuisines: Ethiopian
Average price: Modest
Address: 2109 Avent Ferry Rd
Raleigh, NC 27606
Phone: (919) 664-8151

#301
Sergio's Pizza
Cuisines: Pizza
Average price: Inexpensive
Address: 7440 Louisburg Rd
Raleigh, NC 27616
Phone: (919) 876-3116

#302
Zest Café and Home Art
Cuisines: Breakfast & Brunch, Cafe
Average price: Modest
Address: 8831 Six Forks Rd
Raleigh, NC 27615
Phone: (919) 848-4792

#303
Noodles & Company
Cuisines: Noodles
Average price: Inexpensive
Address: 403 Daniels St
Raleigh, NC 27605
Phone: (919) 755-0282

#304
Sawmill Tap Room
Cuisines: Sports Bar, Burgers, American
Average price: Modest
Address: 7701 Lead Mine Rd
Raleigh, NC 27615
Phone: (919) 845-7889

#305
Salsa Fresh Mexican Grill
Cuisines: Mexican
Average price: Inexpensive
Address: 5910 Duraleigh Rd
Raleigh, NC 27612
Phone: (919) 571-9111

#306
Gypsy's Shiny Diner
Cuisines: Diner, American
Average price: Inexpensive
Address: 1550 Buck Jones Rd
Raleigh, NC 27606
Phone: (919) 469-3663

#307
Big Easy Cajun Crabtree
Cuisines: Cafe
Average price: Inexpensive
Address: 4326 Glenwood Ave
Raleigh, NC 27612
Phone: (919) 786-1733

#308
Chubby's Tacos
Cuisines: Mexican
Average price: Inexpensive
Address: 10511 Shadowlawn Dr, Ste 119
Raleigh, NC 27614
Phone: (919) 846-7044

#309
Deli-icious
Cuisines: Deli, Food Truck
Average price: Inexpensive
Address: 1100 Paine Ct
Raleigh, NC 27609
Phone: (919) 410-8849

#310
Buffalo Brothers Pizza & Wing
Cuisines: American, Pizza, Chicken Wings
Average price: Modest
Address: 3111 Capital Blvd
Raleigh, NC 27604
Phone: (919) 878-4800

#311
Pho 79 & Crawfish
Cuisines: Vietnamese, Seafood
Average price: Modest
Address: 3310 Capital Blvd
Raleigh, NC 27604
Phone: (919) 878-7898

#312
Which Wich
Cuisines: Sandwiches
Average price: Inexpensive
Address: 4120-140 Main at N Hills St
Raleigh, NC 27609
Phone: (919) 786-9111

#313
Mel's BBQ
Cuisines: Barbeque
Average price: Inexpensive
Address: 5008 Forestville Rd
Raleigh, NC 27616
Phone: (919) 872-7855

#314
Nantucket Grill - Raleigh
Cuisines: American, Bakery, Seafood
Average price: Modest
Address: 1145 Falls River Ave
Raleigh, NC 27614
Phone: (919) 870-1955

#315
Mi Rancho
Cuisines: Mexican
Average price: Modest
Address: 2549 S Saunders St
Raleigh, NC 27603
Phone: (919) 836-0807

#316
Café Helios
Cuisines: Cafe, Cocktail Bar
Average price: Inexpensive
Address: 413 Glenwood Ave
Raleigh, NC 27603
Phone: (984) 200-8319

#317
Tripps Restaurant
Cuisines: American, Steakhouse
Average price: Modest
Address: 1428 Garner Station Blvd
Raleigh, NC 27603
Phone: (919) 661-3558

#318
Pogo Cafe
Cuisines: Fast Food, Southern, Deli
Average price: Inexpensive
Address: 201 E Hargett St
Raleigh, NC 27601
Phone: (919) 857-1108

#319
Piccola Italia Pizza & Restaurant
Cuisines: Pizza, Italian
Average price: Modest
Address: 423 Woodburn Rd
Raleigh, NC 27605
Phone: (919) 833-6888

#320
La Rancherita
Cuisines: Mexican
Average price: Modest
Address: 2400 Hillsborough St
Raleigh, NC 27607
Phone: (919) 755-9697

#321
Akari Express
Cuisines: Japanese
Average price: Inexpensive
Address: 2109 Avent Ferry Rd
Raleigh, NC 27606
Phone: (919) 232-5380

#322
Pieology Pizzeria
Cuisines: Pizza
Average price: Inexpensive
Address: 3001 Hillborough St
Raleigh, NC 27607
Phone: (919) 839-6300

#323
Capital Creations Gourmet Pizza
Cuisines: Pizza
Average price: Modest
Address: 1842 Wake Forest Rd
Raleigh, NC 27608
Phone: (919) 836-8000

#324
Salvio's Pizzeria
Cuisines: Chicken Wings, Pizza, Italian
Average price: Inexpensive
Address: 6325 Falls of Neuse Rd
Raleigh, NC 27615
Phone: (919) 981-5678

#325
Simply Crepes
Cuisines: Creperie, Salad, Soup
Average price: Modest
Address: 8470 Honeycutt Rd
Raleigh, NC 27615
Phone: (919) 322-2327

#326
Lemongrass Thai Restaurant
Cuisines: Thai
Average price: Modest
Address: 8320 Litchford Rd
Raleigh, NC 27615
Phone: (919) 954-0377

#327
Fleming's Prime Steakhouse
Cuisines: Steakhouse, Wine Bar
Average price: Exclusive
Address: 4325 Glenwood Ave
Raleigh, NC 27612
Phone: (919) 571-6200

#328
Brixx Wood Fired Pizza
Cuisines: Pizza
Average price: Modest
Address: 8511 Brier Creek Pkwy
Raleigh, NC 27617
Phone: (919) 246-0640

#329
Milton's Pizza-Six Forks
Cuisines: Pizza
Average price: Modest
Address: 8853 Six Forks Rd
Raleigh, NC 27615
Phone: (919) 847-0604

#330
NC Seafood Restaurant
Cuisines: Seafood, Soup, Sandwiches
Average price: Modest
Address: 1201 Agriculture St
Raleigh, NC 27603
Phone: (919) 833-4661

#331
Jubala Village Coffee
Cuisines: Coffee & Tea, Breakfast & Brunch
Average price: Inexpensive
Address: 8450 Honeycutt Rd
Raleigh, NC 27615
Phone: (919) 758-8330

#332
East Village Grill & Bar
Cuisines: Bar, American
Average price: Modest
Address: 1 Dixie Trl
Raleigh, NC 27607
Phone: (919) 821-9985

#333
Chuck & Buck Cones N Cups
Cuisines: Desserts, Ice Cream, Soup
Average price: Inexpensive
Address: 4610 Capital Blvd
Raleigh, NC 27604
Phone: (919) 887-2992

#334
The Peddler Steak House
Cuisines: Steakhouse
Average price: Expensive
Address: 6005 Glenwood Ave
Raleigh, NC 27612
Phone: (919) 787-6980

#335
Cook Out
Cuisines: Burgers, Fast Food
Average price: Inexpensive
Address: 3930 Western Blvd
Raleigh, NC 27606
Phone: (919) 821-2926

#336
Caffe Luna
Cuisines: Italian
Average price: Modest
Address: 136 E Hargett St
Raleigh, NC 27601
Phone: (919) 832-6090

#337
Sushi Blues Cafe
Cuisines: Sushi Bar
Average price: Modest
Address: 301 Glenwood Ave
Raleigh, NC 27603
Phone: (919) 664-8061

#338
Sushi O Bistro and Sushi Bar
Cuisines: Sushi Bar
Average price: Modest
Address: 222 Glenwood Ave
Raleigh, NC 27603
Phone: (919) 838-8868

#339
Carolina Ale House
Cuisines: Sports Bar, American
Average price: Modest
Address: 500 Glenwood Ave
Raleigh, NC 27603
Phone: (919) 835-2222

#340
Iris
Cuisines: American, Breakfast & Brunch
Average price: Modest
Address: 2110 Blue Ridge Rd
Raleigh, NC 27607
Phone: (919) 664-6838

#341
zpizza
Cuisines: Pizza
Average price: Modest
Address: 421 Fayetteville St
Raleigh, NC 27601
Phone: (919) 838-0681

#342
Dantes Italiano
Cuisines: Italian, Pizza
Average price: Modest
Address: 13200 New Falls of Neuse Rd
Raleigh, NC 27614
Phone: (919) 556-2146

#343
Tuscan Blu
Cuisines: Italian, Beer, Wine & Spirits
Average price: Modest
Address: 327 W Davie St
Raleigh, NC 27601
Phone: (919) 834-5707

#344
Woody's At City Market
Cuisines: Sports Bar, Chicken Wings
Average price: Modest
Address: 205 Wolfe St
Raleigh, NC 27601
Phone: (919) 833-3000

#345
San Jose's Tacos & Tequila
Cuisines: Mexican
Average price: Modest
Address: 7961 Skyland Ridge Pkwy
Raleigh, NC 27617
Phone: (919) 957-1400

#346
Amedeo's Italian Restaurant
Cuisines: Italian, Desserts, Salad
Average price: Modest
Address: 3905 Western Blvd
Raleigh, NC 27606
Phone: (919) 851-0473

#347
Chick-fil-A
Cuisines: Fast Food
Average price: Inexpensive
Address: 3770 Lake Boone Trail
Raleigh, NC 27607
Phone: (919) 420-2471

#348
McAlister's Deli
Cuisines: Sandwiches, Deli, Salad
Average price: Inexpensive
Address: 4361 Lassiter Ave
Raleigh, NC 27609
Phone: (919) 787-9543

#349
Penn Station East Coast Subs
Cuisines: Sandwiches
Average price: Inexpensive
Address: 6301-B Falls of Neuse Rd
Raleigh, NC 27609
Phone: (919) 896-6871

#350
Jerk Masters
Cuisines: Caribbean
Average price: Inexpensive
Address: 1909 Poole Rd
Raleigh, NC 27610
Phone: (919) 231-7697

#351
Crazy Fire Mongolian Grill & Sushi
Cuisines: Mongolian
Average price: Modest
Address: 3611 Spring Forest Rd
Raleigh, NC 27616
Phone: (919) 872-3575

#352
Bedford Bistro & Bar
Cuisines: Bar, American, Italian
Average price: Modest
Address: 3607 Falls River Ave
Raleigh, NC 27614
Phone: (919) 720-4482

#353
Chipotle Mexican Grill
Cuisines: Mexican, Fast Food
Average price: Inexpensive
Address: 2316 Hillsborough St
Raleigh, NC 27607
Phone: (919) 576-1894

#354
Red Hot & Blue
Cuisines: Barbeque, Bar, Seafood
Average price: Modest
Address: 6615 Falls of Neuse Rd
Raleigh, NC 27615
Phone: (919) 846-7427

#355
**Seven Cities Seafood
& Southern Cuisine**
Cuisines: Seafood
Average price: Inexpensive
Address: 3611 Spring Forest Rd
Raleigh, NC 27616
Phone: (919) 307-4297

#356
Farina Neighborhood Italian
Cuisines: Pizza, Italian, Breakfast & Brunch
Average price: Modest
Address: 8450 Honeycutt Rd
Raleigh, NC 27615
Phone: (919) 890-0143

#357
La Cocina De Mama Greta
Cuisines: Salvadoran
Average price: Inexpensive
Address: 1604 N Market Dr
Raleigh, NC 27609
Phone: (919) 872-5360

#358
Sushi One
Cuisines: Sushi Bar, Asian Fusion, Japanese
Average price: Modest
Address: 8470 Honeycutt Rd
Raleigh, NC 27615
Phone: (919) 615-3209

#359
New World Coffee House
Cuisines: Coffee & Tea, Sandwiches,
Breakfast & Brunch
Average price: Inexpensive
Address: 4112 Pleasant Valley Rd
Raleigh, NC 27612
Phone: (919) 786-0091

#360
Stromboli's
Cuisines: Italian, Pizza
Average price: Modest
Address: 3434 Edwards Mill Rd
Raleigh, NC 27612
Phone: (919) 785-7075

#361
Chipotle Mexican Grill
Cuisines: Mexican, Fast Food
Average price: Inexpensive
Address: 6102 Falls of Neuse Rd
Raleigh, NC 27609
Phone: (919) 877-8544

#362
Uncorked
Cuisines: Wine Bar, Tapas/Small Plates
Average price: Modest
Address: 10511 Shadowlawn Dr
Raleigh, NC 27614
Phone: (919) 847-1530

#363
Brigs Great Beginnings
Cuisines: Breakfast & Brunch, Sandwiches
Average price: Inexpensive
Address: 8111 Creedmoor Rd
Raleigh, NC 27613
Phone: (919) 870-0994

#364
Tasca Brava
Cuisines: Spanish, Tapas Bar,
Latin American
Average price: Expensive
Address: 607 Glenwood Ave
Raleigh, NC 27603
Phone: (919) 828-0840

#365
Kick Back Jack's
Cuisines: Fast Food
Average price: Modest
Address: 1405 Garner Station Blvd
Raleigh, NC 27603
Phone: (919) 803-5068

#366
Edwards Mill Bar & Grill
Cuisines: Bar, American
Average price: Modest
Address: 3201 Edwards Mill Rd
Raleigh, NC 27612
Phone: (919) 783-5447

#367
Golden Dragon
Cuisines: Chinese
Average price: Inexpensive
Address: 2402 Hillsborough St
Raleigh, NC 27607
Phone: (919) 834-2626

#368
Wingstop
Cuisines: Chicken Wings
Average price: Modest
Address: 1721 New Hope Church Rd
Raleigh, NC 27609
Phone: (919) 872-8856

#369
Grandotes Taco Grill
Cuisines: Food Truck, Mexican
Average price: Inexpensive
Address: 1025 Blue Ridge Rd
Raleigh, NC 27607
Phone: (919) 306-1656

#370
El Taco Market
Cuisines: Mexican
Average price: Inexpensive
Address: 3800 New Bern Ave
Raleigh, NC 27610
Phone: (919) 250-0412

#371
Jerry's Grill
Cuisines: Fast Food
Average price: Inexpensive
Address: 813 E Whitaker Mill Rd
Raleigh, NC 27608
Phone: (919) 832-7561

#372
Mash and Lauter
Cuisines: Belgian, Beer Bar
Average price: Modest
Address: 225 S Wilmington St
Raleigh, NC 27601
Phone: (919) 833-1133

#373
Sola Coffee Cafe
Cuisines: Cafe, Donuts
Average price: Inexpensive
Address: 7705 Lead Mine Rd
Raleigh, NC 27615
Phone: (919) 803-8983

#374
Around the World Market
Cuisines: Indian, Grocery, Imported Food
Average price: Inexpensive
Address: 6715 Hillsborough St
Raleigh, NC 27606
Phone: (919) 859-5403

#375
Crepe Traditions
Cuisines: Creperie, Coffee & Tea,
Breakfast & Brunch
Average price: Inexpensive
Address: 141 Park At N Hills St
Raleigh, NC 27609
Phone: (919) 977-3425

#376
Las Margaritas Mexican Restaurant II
Cuisines: Mexican
Average price: Inexpensive
Address: 7431 6 Forks Rd
Raleigh, NC 27615
Phone: (919) 847-6438

#377
Pullen Place
Cuisines: Sandwiches, Gluten-Free, Soup
Average price: Inexpensive
Address: 520 Ashe Ave
Raleigh, NC 27606
Phone: (919) 829-7180

#378
The Cheesecake Factory
Cuisines: American, Desserts
Average price: Modest
Address: 4325 Glenwood Ave
Raleigh, NC 27612
Phone: (919) 781-0050

#379
Peace China
Cuisines: Chinese
Average price: Inexpensive
Address: 802 Semart Dr
Raleigh, NC 27604
Phone: (919) 833-8668

#380
Golden Seafood & Chicken
Cuisines: Chicken Wings
Average price: Inexpensive
Address: 2600 S Saunders St
Raleigh, NC 27603
Phone: (919) 833-0121

#381
Stonehenge Tavern
Cuisines: Burgers, American, Sandwiches
Average price: Modest
Address: 7504 Creedmoor Rd
Raleigh, NC 27613
Phone: (919) 676-0332

#382
Cloos' Coney Island
Cuisines: Hot Dogs, Burgers
Average price: Inexpensive
Address: 2233 Avent Ferry Rd
Raleigh, NC 27606
Phone: (919) 834-3354

#383
Shane's Rib Shack
Cuisines: Barbeque
Average price: Modest
Address: 5811 Poyner Village Pkwy
Raleigh, NC 27616
Phone: (919) 850-9900

#384
Trali Irish Pub & Restaurant
Cuisines: Pub, Irish
Average price: Modest
Address: 10370 Moncreiffe Rd
Raleigh, NC 27617
Phone: (919) 544-4141

#385
Chick-fil-A
Cuisines: Fast Food
Average price: Inexpensive
Address: 4154 Main North Hills St
Raleigh, NC 27609
Phone: (919) 510-0100

#386
Wang's Kitchen
Cuisines: Chinese
Average price: Modest
Address: 4701 Atlantic Ave
Raleigh, NC 27604
Phone: (919) 878-5578

#387
Salsa Fresh Mexican Grill
Cuisines: Mexican
Average price: Inexpensive
Address: 9650 Strickland Rd
Raleigh, NC 27615
Phone: (919) 870-1107

#388
Snoopy's Hot Dogs & More
Cuisines: Hot Dogs
Average price: Inexpensive
Address: 1931 Wake Forest Rd
Raleigh, NC 27608
Phone: (919) 833-0992

#389
Mizu
Cuisines: Sushi Bar, Japanese
Average price: Modest
Address: 10750 Wakefield Commons Dr
Raleigh, NC 27614
Phone: (919) 453-2875

#390
Tokyo House
Cuisines: Japanese, Sushi Bar, Thai
Average price: Modest
Address: 7439 Six Forks Rd
Raleigh, NC 27615
Phone: (919) 848-3350

#391
Tilted Kilt Pub & Eatery
Cuisines: American, Sports Bar, Pub
Average price: Modest
Address: 4516 Falls Of Neuse Rd.
Raleigh, NC 27609
Phone: (919) 790-8898

#392
Checkers Pizza & Subs
Cuisines: Pizza
Average price: Inexpensive
Address: 2810 Hillsborough St
Raleigh, NC 27607
Phone: (919) 832-6255

#393
Jason's Deli
Cuisines: Sandwiches, Deli
Average price: Inexpensive
Address: 909 Spring Forest Rd
Raleigh, NC 27609
Phone: (919) 855-9898

#394
Stromboli's
Cuisines: Italian, Pizza
Average price: Modest
Address: 2900 Spring Forest Rd
Raleigh, NC 27616
Phone: (919) 876-4222

#395
Pharaoh's
Cuisines: Burgers, Sandwiches, Fast Food
Average price: Inexpensive
Address: 4421 Six Forks Rd
Raleigh, NC 27609
Phone: (919) 420-0840

#396
High Park Bar & Grill
Cuisines: Sports Bar, American
Average price: Modest
Address: 625 E Whitaker Mill Rd
Raleigh, NC 27608
Phone: (919) 833-4527

#397
Bruno Restaurant
Cuisines: Seafood, Steakhouse, Italian
Average price: Expensive
Address: 11211 Galleria Ave
Raleigh, NC 27614
Phone: (919) 435-6640

#398
Hayashi Japanese Restaurant
Cuisines: Sushi Bar, Japanese
Average price: Modest
Address: 13200 New Falls Of Neuse Rd
Raleigh, NC 27614
Phone: (919) 554-0508

#399
Cook Out
Cuisines: Burgers, Hot Dogs, Fast Food
Average price: Inexpensive
Address: 3244 Capital Blvd
Raleigh, NC 27604
Phone: (919) 862-8280

#400
Baja Burrito
Cuisines: Mexican
Average price: Inexpensive
Address: 2109 Avent Ferry Rd
Raleigh, NC 27606
Phone: (919) 834-3431

#401
b.good
Cuisines: Salad, Burgers, Sandwiches
Average price: Modest
Address: 555 Fayetteville st
Raleigh, NC 27601
Phone: (919) 803-3233

#402
China Won
Cuisines: Chinese
Average price: Inexpensive
Address: 8109 Fayetteville Rd
Raleigh, NC 27603
Phone: (919) 662-9799

#403
Chai's Asian Bistro
Cuisines: Asian Fusion
Average price: Modest
Address: 8347 Creedmoor Rd
Raleigh, NC 27613
Phone: (919) 341-3715

#404
Char-Grill
Cuisines: Burgers
Average price: Inexpensive
Address: 4621 Atlantic Ave
Raleigh, NC 27604
Phone: (919) 954-9556

#405
San Jose Mexican Restaurant
Cuisines: Mexican
Average price: Modest
Address: 5811 Poyner Village Pkwy
Raleigh, NC 27616
Phone: (919) 790-1919

#406
Tamarind
Cuisines: Asian Fusion, Vegetarian
Average price: Inexpensive
Address: 8531 Brier Creek Pkwy
Raleigh, NC 27617
Phone: (919) 406-3473

#407
Thai Villa
Cuisines: Thai, Vegetarian
Average price: Modest
Address: 1319 Buck Jones Rd
Raleigh, NC 27606
Phone: (919) 462-9010

#408
Beansprout Chinese Restaurant
Cuisines: Chinese
Average price: Inexpensive
Address: 3721 Hillsborough St
Raleigh, NC 27607
Phone: (919) 755-0554

#409
Tropical Smoothie Cafe
Cuisines: Juice Bar, Sandwiches
Average price: Inexpensive
Address: 1028 Oberlin Rd
Raleigh, NC 27605
Phone: (919) 755-2222

#410
Sweet Tomatoes
Cuisines: Vegetarian, Buffet, Salad
Average price: Modest
Address: 5200 Capital Blvd.
Raleigh, NC 27616
Phone: (919) 871-0310

#411
Taste of China
Cuisines: Chinese
Average price: Inexpensive
Address: 6209 Rock Quarry Rd
Raleigh, NC 27610
Phone: (919) 773-2285

#412
Which Wich ?
Cuisines: Sandwiches
Average price: Inexpensive
Address: 4025 Lake Boone Trl
Raleigh, NC 27607
Phone: (919) 781-1101

#413
Dino's Capri Restaurant
Cuisines: Italian
Average price: Modest
Address: 6325 Falls of Neuse Rd
Raleigh, NC 27615
Phone: (919) 878-4424

#414
Crazy Fire Mongolian Grill
Cuisines: Mongolian
Average price: Modest
Address: 1270 Buck Jones Rd
Raleigh, NC 27606
Phone: (919) 481-2222

#415
Waba
Cuisines: Korean
Average price: Inexpensive
Address: 2502 12nd hillsborough St
Raleigh, NC 27607
Phone: (919) 833-1710

#416
Five Guys Burgers and Fries
Cuisines: Fast Food, Burgers
Average price: Inexpensive
Address: 8107 Creedmoor Rd
Raleigh, NC 27613
Phone: (919) 844-7057

#417
Annelore's German Bakery
Cuisines: Bakery, German, Desserts
Average price: Modest
Address: 1249 Farmers Market Dr
Raleigh, NC 27603
Phone: (919) 294-8040

#418
Caribbean Cafe
Cuisines: Caribbean
Average price: Modest
Address: 2645 E Millbrook Rd
Raleigh, NC 27604
Phone: (919) 872-4858

#419
El Rodeo
Cuisines: Mexican, Seafood
Average price: Modest
Address: 4112 Pleasant Valley Rd
Raleigh, NC 27613
Phone: (919) 571-1188

#420
Oishi Japanese Cuisine
Cuisines: Japanese
Average price: Inexpensive
Address: 2526 Hillsborough St
Raleigh, NC 27607
Phone: (919) 322-0828

#421
Global Village Organic Coffee
Cuisines: Coffee & Tea, Sandwiches
Average price: Inexpensive
Address: 2428 Hillsborough St
Raleigh, NC 27607
Phone: (919) 828-4567

#422
Five Guys Famous Burgers
Cuisines: Burgers, Hot Dogs
Average price: Inexpensive
Address: 4120 Main at N Hills St
Raleigh, NC 27609
Phone: (919) 787-7772

#423
Hibachi Japan
Cuisines: Japanese
Average price: Inexpensive
Address: 4001 Wake Forest Rd
Raleigh, NC 27609
Phone: (919) 878-8880

#424
Bangkok Thai
Cuisines: Thai, Salad, Soup
Average price: Modest
Address: 13200 Falls of Neuse Rd
Raleigh, NC 27614
Phone: (919) 554-1561

#425
Peking Garden
Cuisines: Chinese
Average price: Modest
Address: 126 E Millbrook Rd
Raleigh, NC 27609
Phone: (919) 848-4663

#426
Japan Express
Cuisines: Japanese
Average price: Inexpensive
Address: 6250 Glenwood Ave
Raleigh, NC 27612
Phone: (919) 788-7758

#427
Snoopy's Hot Dogs & More
Cuisines: Hot Dogs, Fast Food
Average price: Inexpensive
Address: 600 Hillsborough St
Raleigh, NC 27603
Phone: (919) 839-2176

#428
Kabobi
Cuisines: Mediterranean, Persian/Iranian
Average price: Inexpensive
Address: 4325 Glenwood Ave
Raleigh, NC 27612
Phone: (919) 783-0506

#429
Ruckus Pizza
Cuisines: Pizza, Dive Bar, Music Venue
Average price: Inexpensive
Address: 2233 Avent Ferry Rd
Raleigh, NC 27606
Phone: (919) 835-2002

#430
Toreros Mexican Restaurant
Cuisines: Mexican
Average price: Modest
Address: 4721 Atlantic Ave
Raleigh, NC 27604
Phone: (919) 873-9116

#431
Wang's Kitchen
Cuisines: Chinese
Average price: Modest
Address: 3631 New Bern Ave
Raleigh, NC 27610
Phone: (919) 212-8805

#432
Leesville Tap Room
Cuisines: Bar, American
Average price: Modest
Address: 13200 Strickland Rd
Raleigh, NC 27613
Phone: (919) 870-1515

#433
Steak 'n Shake
Cuisines: Burgers, Fast Food
Average price: Inexpensive
Address: 2840 Millbrook Rd
Raleigh, NC 27604
Phone: (919) 872-6669

#434
Lunches San Luis
Cuisines: Mexican, Food Stands
Average price: Inexpensive
Address: 3622 New Bern Ave
Raleigh, NC 27610
Phone: (919) 337-7949

#435
Hooters
Cuisines: American, Chicken Wings
Average price: Modest
Address: 4206 Wake Forest Rd
Raleigh, NC 27609
Phone: (919) 850-9882

#436
Bull and the Bear
Cuisines: American, Pub
Average price: Inexpensive
Address: Colony Shopping Ctr
Raleigh, NC 27601
Phone: (919) 847-3617

#437
The Club House Restaurant
Cuisines: American, Bar
Average price: Inexpensive
Address: 42 40 Garner
Raleigh, NC 27601
Phone: (919) 662-2207

#438
El Rodeo Mexican Restaurant
Cuisines: Mexican
Average price: Inexpensive
Address: 2404 Wake Forest Rd
Raleigh, NC 27608
Phone: (919) 833-1460

#439
Carolina Ale House
Cuisines: Sports Bar, American
Average price: Modest
Address: 7981 Skyland Ridge Pkwy
Raleigh, NC 27617
Phone: (919) 957-4200

#440
Sake House
Cuisines: Sushi Bar
Average price: Modest
Address: 1141 Falls River Ave
Raleigh, NC 27614
Phone: (919) 676-5788

#441
Shanghai Express
Cuisines: Chinese, Thai
Average price: Inexpensive
Address: 2502 Hillsborough St
Raleigh, NC 27607
Phone: (919) 754-9797

#442
Italian Kitchen Pizza & Grill
Cuisines: Italian, Pizza, Sandwiches
Average price: Inexpensive
Address: 4005 Wake Forest Rd
Raleigh, NC 27609
Phone: (919) 790-2444

#443
Kanki
Cuisines: Japanese, Sushi Bar
Average price: Modest
Address: 4500 Old Wake Forest Rd
Raleigh, NC 27609
Phone: (919) 876-4157

#444
Hungry Howie's Pizza
Cuisines: Pizza
Average price: Inexpensive
Address: 6701 Glenwood Ave
Raleigh, NC 27612
Phone: (919) 782-3434

#445
Bella Italia
Cuisines: Italian, Pizza
Average price: Modest
Address: 10630 Durant Rd
Raleigh, NC 27614
Phone: (919) 676-0076

#446
Kanki
Cuisines: Japanese, Sushi Bar, Steakhouse
Average price: Modest
Address: 4325 Glenwood Ave
Raleigh, NC 27612
Phone: (919) 782-9708

#447
Peace China
Cuisines: Chinese
Average price: Inexpensive
Address: 13220 Strickland Rd
Raleigh, NC 27613
Phone: (919) 676-9968

#448
Crisp Salads
Cuisines: Sandwiches, Salad
Average price: Inexpensive
Address: 4325 Glenwood Ave
Raleigh, NC 27612
Phone: (919) 787-9257

#449
Five Guys Burgers and Fries
Cuisines: Burgers, Hot Dogs, Sandwiches
Average price: Modest
Address: 5501 Capital Blvd
Raleigh, NC 27616
Phone: (984) 232-0547

#450
Cook Out
Cuisines: Fast Food
Average price: Inexpensive
Address: 6505 Falls of Neuse Rd
Raleigh, NC 27615
Phone: (919) 862-8830

#451
Hibachi China Buffet
Cuisines: Chinese, Buffet
Average price: Modest
Address: 2909 E Millbrook Rd
Raleigh, NC 27616
Phone: (919) 878-5688

#452
Pei Wei
Cuisines: Gluten-Free, Asian Fusion
Average price: Inexpensive
Address: 10251 Little Brier Creek Ln
Raleigh, NC 27617
Phone: (919) 484-4113

#453
Ba-da Wings
Cuisines: Chicken Wings
Average price: Inexpensive
Address: 2161 Avent Ferry Rd
Raleigh, NC 27617
Phone: (919) 832-3902

#454
Petra Grill
Cuisines: Mediterranean, Greek
Average price: Inexpensive
Address: 6091 Capital Blvd
Raleigh, NC 27616
Phone: (919) 599-4959

#455
Backyard Burger
Cuisines: Burgers
Average price: Inexpensive
Address: 9860 Leesville Rd
Raleigh, NC 27613
Phone: (919) 847-7098

#456
Shish Kabob
Cuisines: Mediterranean, Vegetarian, Greek
Average price: Inexpensive
Address: 9101 Leesville Rd
Raleigh, NC 27613
Phone: (919) 848-1211

#457
Hibachi Grill and Supreme Buffet
Cuisines: Buffet, Chinese, Sushi Bar
Average price: Inexpensive
Address: 3131 Capital Blvd
Raleigh, NC 27604
Phone: (919) 878-5888

#458
Dickey's Barbecue Pit
Cuisines: Barbeque
Average price: Modest
Address: 6552 Glenwood Ave
Raleigh, NC 27613
Phone: (919) 436-3995

#459
La Rancherita
Cuisines: Mexican
Average price: Modest
Address: 7420 6 Forks Rd
Raleigh, NC 27615
Phone: (919) 844-6330

#460
Kings North Hills
Cuisines: American, Bowling, Sports Bar
Average price: Modest
Address: 141 Park At North Hills St
Raleigh, NC 27609
Phone: (919) 600-5700

#461
Torii Noodle Bar
Cuisines: Japanese, Noodles
Average price: Modest
Address: 4325 Glenwood Ave
Raleigh, NC 27612
Phone: (919) 782-9708

#462
Char-Grill Two
Cuisines: Burgers
Average price: Inexpensive
Address: 3211 Edwards Mill Rd
Raleigh, NC 27612
Phone: (919) 781-2945

#463
Chipotle Mexican Grill
Cuisines: Mexican, Fast Food
Average price: Inexpensive
Address: 6602 Glenwood Ave
Raleigh, NC 27612
Phone: (919) 781-5115

#464
I Love Ny Pizza
Cuisines: Pizza
Average price: Inexpensive
Address: 2316 Hillsborough St
Raleigh, NC 27607
Phone: (919) 838-0011

#465
Jade Garden Chinese Restaurant
Cuisines: Chinese
Average price: Inexpensive
Address: 1207 Hillsborough St
Raleigh, NC 27603
Phone: (919) 594-1813

#466
Lam's Garden
Cuisines: Cafe
Average price: Modest
Address: 1100 N Raleigh Blvd
Raleigh, NC 27610
Phone: (919) 828-2118

#467
Milton's Pizza-Wakefield
Cuisines: Pizza, Italian, Salad
Average price: Modest
Address: 14520 New Falls Of Neuse
Raleigh, NC 27614
Phone: (919) 570-9099

#468
Jasmin Mediterranean Bistro
Cuisines: Mediterranean, Greek, Lebanese
Average price: Inexpensive
Address: 2430 Hillsborough St
Raleigh, NC 27607
Phone: (919) 755-9991

#469
**McCormick & Schmick's
Seafood & Steaks**
Cuisines: Seafood
Average price: Expensive
Address: 4325 Glenwood Ave
Raleigh, NC 27612
Phone: (919) 881-7848

#470
Sami's Subs, Pizza, and More
Cuisines: Pizza, Sandwiches
Average price: Inexpensive
Address: 6405 Westgate Rd
Raleigh, NC 27617
Phone: (919) 571-8555

#471
Char-Grill
Cuisines: Burgers
Average price: Inexpensive
Address: 9601 Strickland Rd
Raleigh, NC 27609
Phone: (919) 845-8994

#472
Brasa Brazilian Steakhouse
Cuisines: Brazilian, Steakhouse
Average price: Expensive
Address: 8551 Brier Creek Pkwy
Raleigh, NC 27617
Phone: (919) 544-3344

#473
Jasmin Mediterranean Bistro
Cuisines: Mediterranean, Greek, Lebanese
Average price: Inexpensive
Address: 424 E Six Forks Rd
Raleigh, NC 27609
Phone: (919) 743-3336

#474
Redbowl Asian Bistro
Cuisines: Asian Fusion, Sushi Bar
Average price: Modest
Address: 6360 Plantation Center Dr
Raleigh, NC 27616
Phone: (919) 790-9222

#475
Champa Thai & Sushi Restaurant
Cuisines: Sushi Bar, Thai
Average price: Modest
Address: 8521 Brier Creek Pkwy
Raleigh, NC 27617
Phone: (919) 806-0078

#476
Sub Conscious
Cuisines: Sandwiches
Average price: Inexpensive
Address: 3209 Hillsborough St
Raleigh, NC 27607
Phone: (919) 833-3535

#477
Jersey Mike's Subs
Cuisines: Sandwiches, Fast Food, Deli
Average price: Inexpensive
Address: 4121-101 New Bern Avenue
Raleigh, NC 27610
Phone: (919) 231-0070

#478
Kome Asian Cuisine
Cuisines: Chinese, Sushi Bar
Average price: Modest
Address: 4551 New Bern Ave
Raleigh, NC 27610
Phone: (919) 212-6666

#479
Skybox Grill & Bar
Cuisines: Sports Bar, American
Average price: Modest
Address: 3415 Wake Forest Rd
Raleigh, NC 27609
Phone: (919) 878-4917

#480
Jet's Pizza
Cuisines: Pizza
Average price: Inexpensive
Address: 3004 Wake Forest Rd
Raleigh, NC 27609
Phone: (919) 877-8660

#481
Biscuitville
Cuisines: Southern
Average price: Inexpensive
Address: 2426 Wake Forest Rd
Raleigh, NC 27608
Phone: (919) 821-2060

#482
El Rey del Taco
Cuisines: Food Truck, Mexican
Average price: Inexpensive
Address: 1700 St Albans Dr
Raleigh, NC 27608
Phone: (919) 908-4665

#483
Fitzgerald's Seafood
Cuisines: Seafood, Barbeque
Average price: Modest
Address: 3400 New Birch Dr
Raleigh, NC 27610
Phone: (919) 803-3451

#484
The Melting Pot
Cuisines: Fondue
Average price: Expensive
Address: 3100 Wake Forest Rd
Raleigh, NC 27609
Phone: (919) 878-0477

#485
Korner Pocket
Cuisines: Sports Bar, American
Average price: Modest
Address: 8508 Capital Blvd
Raleigh, NC 27616
Phone: (919) 876-9879

#486
Neo-Asia Restaurant
Cuisines: Chinese, Asian Fusion
Average price: Modest
Address: 6602 Glenwood Ave
Raleigh, NC 27612
Phone: (919) 783-8383

#487
Cafe Capistrano
Cuisines: Mexican, Cafe
Average price: Modest
Address: 8741 Garvey Dr
Raleigh, NC 27616
Phone: (919) 872-1127

#488
Barbecue Lodge
Cuisines: Barbeque
Average price: Inexpensive
Address: 4600 Capital Blvd
Raleigh, NC 27604
Phone: (919) 872-4755

#489
Los Tres Magueyes
Cuisines: Mexican
Average price: Modest
Address: 10410 Moncreiffe Rd
Raleigh, NC 27617
Phone: (919) 484-9258

#490
Cook Out
Cuisines: Burgers
Average price: Inexpensive
Address: 3210 S Wilmington St
Raleigh, NC 27603
Phone: (919) 661-5801

#491
Circus Family Restaurant
Cuisines: American, Hot Dogs
Average price: Inexpensive
Address: 1600 Wake Forest Rd
Raleigh, NC 27604
Phone: (919) 834-2213

#492
Jason's Deli
Cuisines: Deli, Sandwiches, Salad
Average price: Inexpensive
Address: 8421 Brier Creek Pkwy
Raleigh, NC 27617
Phone: (919) 572-9996

#493
Almadina Supermarket
Cuisines: Grocery, Mediterranean
Average price: Inexpensive
Address: 1019 Method Rd
Raleigh, NC 27606
Phone: (919) 755-6220

#494
Crosswinds Cafe
Cuisines: American, Caterer
Average price: Inexpensive
Address: 1750 E Intenational Blvd
Raleigh, NC 27623
Phone: (919) 840-7625

#495
Bojangles
Cuisines: Fast Food, Chicken Wings
Average price: Inexpensive
Address: 3808 Western Blvd
Raleigh, NC 27606
Phone: (919) 664-8613

#496
D P Dough
Cuisines: Pizza, Fast Food
Average price: Inexpensive
Address: 2109 Avent Ferry Rd
Raleigh, NC 27606
Phone: (919) 829-1525

#497
StarBar
Cuisines: Lounge, Soul Food, Caribbean
Average price: Modest
Address: 1731 Trawick Rd
Raleigh, NC 27604
Phone: (919) 231-3535

#498
Rudino's Sports Corner
Cuisines: Sandwiches, Pizza, Sports Bar
Average price: Modest
Address: 3101-101 Edwards Mill Rd
Raleigh, NC 27612
Phone: (919) 786-4235

#499
The Gourmet Factory
Cuisines: Italian
Average price: Modest
Address: 3933 Western Blvd
Raleigh, NC 27606
Phone: (919) 852-2223

#500
The Original NY Pizza
Cuisines: Pizza
Average price: Inexpensive
Address: 6679 Falls of Neuse Rd, Ste 103
Raleigh, NC 27615
Phone: (919) 841-5999

Made in the USA
Middletown, DE
07 December 2021

54560318R00027